SAMPLER

LEARN AND COLOR BOOKS
Fulton, KY

Current and upcoming titles:

Learn and Color Nature Series
- Medicinal Herbs
- Freshwater Fish
- Garden Edibles

Learn and Color Stained Glass Series
- Landscapes & Seascapes
- Fish & Fowl
- Flowers

People Series, Events Series, and Places Series
- Early Civilization
- The Ancient World
- The Middle Ages
- The Renaissance and Reformation
- The Industrial Revolution
- The Modern Age
- The Computer Age

Learn and Color Sampler
© 2019 Master Design Marketing, LLC

All rights reserved. This book or parts thereof may not be reproduced in any form, stored in any retrieval system, or transmitted in any form by any means—electronic, mechanical, photocopy, recording, or otherwise—without prior written permission of the publisher, except as provided by United States of America copyright law. For permission requests, write to the publisher, at "Permissions Coordinator," at the address below.

Learn & Color Books
 an imprint of Master Design Marketing, LLC
 789 State Route 94 E
 Fulton, KY 42041
 www.LearnAndColor.com

For information about special discounts available for bulk purchases, sales promotions, fund-raising and educational needs, contact Learn & Color Books Company Sales at sales@LearnAndColor.com.

ISBN: 978-1-947482-21-0

Important. Please Read: This book is for the presentation of vegetables, herbs, and fish and its contents are for informational purposes only. Never consume any plant without first consulting your doctor. Never take any plant without your doctor's consent if you are pregnant, nursing, or trying to get pregnant. Never give vegetables to children without first talking to their doctor. The statements made in this book have not been evaluated by the FDA. The vegetables and herbs mentioned are not intended to cure, treat, diagnose or prevent disease. They make us say this.

Cover and interior design by Faithe F Thomas
Research by Caitlyn F Williams
Hardiness Maps © USDA (https://planthardiness.ars.usda.gov/PHZMWeb/Downloads.aspx)
All other Photos and Illustrations © 123RF
Text in this book is a derivative of information by Wikipedia.com, used under CC BY 4.0.
The text of this book is licensed under CC BY 4.0 by Faithe F Thomas.

Pages in this book come from:

Learn and Color Nature Series
Garden Edibles
Medicinal Herbs
Freshwater Fish

Early Civilization
The Industrial Revolution

Learn and Color Stained Glass Series
Fish & Fowl

Pumpkin
Cucurbita pepo

Description

Part of the winter squash family, pumpkins are a vine vegetable that crave lots of warmth and sunlight. They produce both a male and female flower, and honeybees play a significant role in fertilization. Pumpkins have many health benefits, and are perfect for the cooler months when we tend to get sick.

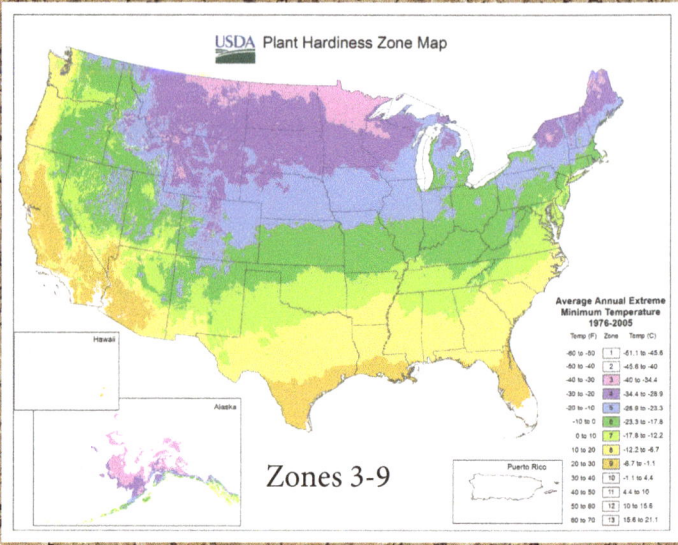

Zones 3-9

Seeding Square Template

4+ square feet per plant

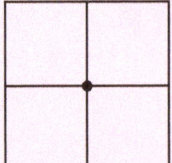

Times to Plant

Ideal soil temperature for pumpkin seeds is 95°, so wait until your soil temperatures are a minimum of 70° before directly planting seeds in your garden. They require at least 100 days of frost-free growing.

Companion Plants

Datura, corn, pole beans

Pumpkin

Echinacea
Echinacea purpurea

Important Facts

- Very popular for treating colds and flu.
- A great immune system booster.
- Enjoyed as a healthy tea.
- Used for sore throat and upper respiratory tract infections.
- A good detoxifier and has antiviral, anti-inflammatory and antibiotic properties.
- Echinacea purpurea is an herbaceous perennial up to 47 in tall by 10 in wide at maturity.
- Slugs eat this plant. Rabbits will also eat the foliage when young, or shortly after emerging in the spring.

Common Names

Purple coneflower, coneflower, purple encinacea

Parts Used

Roots, leaves and flowers

Habitat

Echinacea is native to Central and Eastern North America

Cautions

Side effects include gastrointestinal effects and allergic reactions, including rashes, increased asthma, and life-threatening anaphylaxis.

Other Information

In indigenous medicine of the native American Indians, the plant was used externally for wounds, burns, and insect bites, chewing of roots for toothache and throat infections; internal application was used for pain, cough, stomach cramps, and snake bites.

It is purported that all parts of the purple coneflower stimulate the immune system.

Redbreast Sunfish
Lepomis auritus

Description
Commonly mistaken for a bluegill, redbreast sunfish are popular with anglers. They are also kept as an aquarium fish by hobbyists. Their meat is commonly dipped in batter and fried. They bite at almost anything, so they are commonly caught, along with bluegill and catfish.

Region
The species native range is condensed to eastern North America, in Canada and south to the rivers emptying into the Atlantic Ocean. The species has been introduced as far west as Texas.

Habitat
The redbreast thrives in streams and rivers with shelter and structure, usually around banks with the water pH around 7.0-7.5. It tends to be more of a cool-river species, but also inhabits freshwater lakes and streams. They prefer areas with slow-moving or sluggish water.

Key Indication Marks
The redbreast's body is a bluish-green that fades into a bright orange-yellow belly in females, and a deep orange-red belly in males. Both males and females have vertical rows of red-brown to orange spots on the sides of the body. The operculum, or gill cover, has a distinguishing long black lobe. In adults, the lobe often reaches a length of one inch or more; it is narrow and usually not wider than the eye.

Tips to Catch
Redbreast is popular with fly anglers in the winter because it will more readily strike a moving fly than will bluegills in cooler water. They will attack surface lures without hesitation.

Lures to Use
Live bait, such as nightcrawlers, crickets, grasshoppers, waxworms, or mealworms. Small lures or flies also work.

Easy to Catch

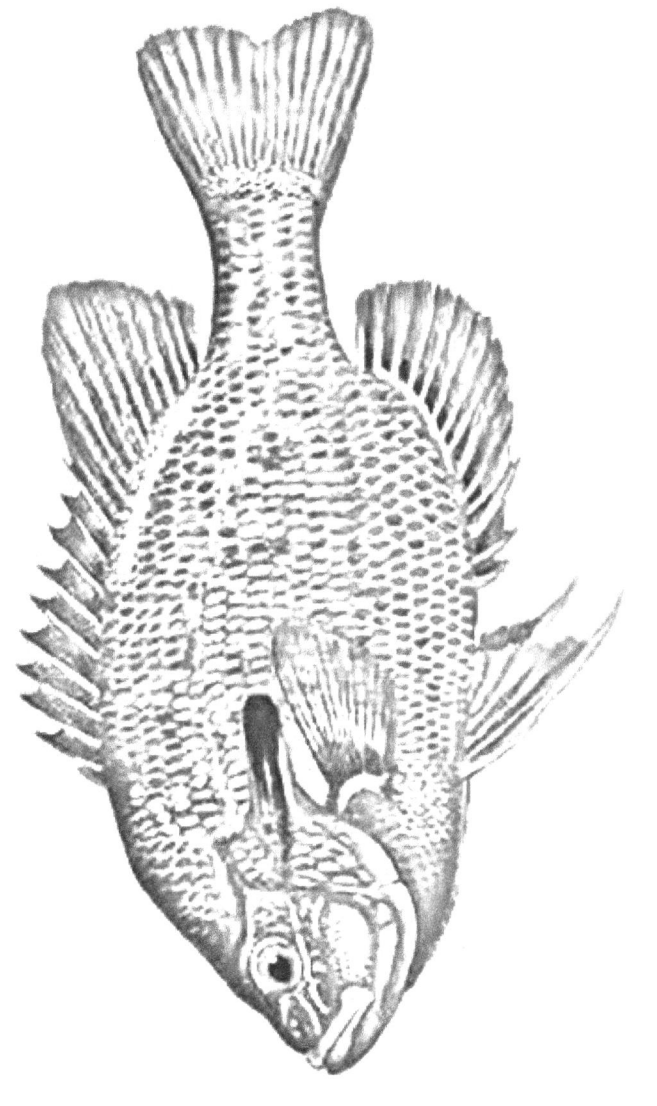

Redbreast Sunfish

Daniel prays to his God

Daniel (c. 620–538 BC) was a noble Jewish youth of Jerusalem, who was taken into captivity by Nebuchadnezzar II of Babylon and served the king and his successors with loyalty and ability until the time of the Persian conqueror Cyrus, all the while remaining true to the God of Israel.

Nebuchadnezzar II dreamed of a giant statue made of four metals with feet of mingled iron and clay, smashed by a stone from heaven. Only Daniel was able to interpret it: the dream signified four kingdoms, of which Babylon was the first, but God would destroy them and replace them with His own kingdom.

Darius, the next ruler, elevated Daniel to high office, exciting the jealousy of other officials. Knowing of Daniel's devotion to his God, his enemies tricked the king into issuing an edict forbidding worship of any other god or man for a 30-day period. Daniel continued to pray three times a day to God towards Jerusalem. He was accused and King Darius, forced by his own decree, threw Daniel into the lions' den. But God shut up the mouths of the lions, and the next morning Darius rejoiced to find him unharmed. The king cast Daniel's accusers into the lions' pit together with their wives and children to be devoured, while Darius acknowledged Daniel's God as the One whose kingdom shall never be destroyed.

The Book of Daniel records these and other events in Daniel's life, including the story of three of his companions being thrown into the fiery furnace. This book belongs not only to the religious tradition but also to the wider Western intellectual and artistic heritage. It was easily the most popular of the prophetic books for the Anglo-Saxons, who nevertheless treated it not as prophecy but as an historical book.

DANIEL

THALES

700 BC   600 BC   500 BC

Abraham Lincoln (1809-1865) was an American lawyer and politician who served as the 16th president of the United States from 1861 until his assassination in April 1865. Lincoln led the nation through the American Civil War, its bloodiest war and its greatest moral, constitutional, and political crisis. He preserved the Union, abolished slavery, strengthened the federal government, and modernized the U.S. economy.

Born in Kentucky, Lincoln grew up on the frontier in a poor family. Self-educated, he became a lawyer, Whig Party leader, state legislator, and Congressman. He left government to resume his law practice, but reentered politics in 1854. He ran for President in 1860, sweeping the North and winning. Southern pro-slavery elements took his win as proof that the North was rejecting the Constitutional rights of Southern states to practice slavery. They began the process of seceding from the union. Lincoln called up volunteers and militia to suppress the rebellion and restore the Union. His Gettysburg Address became an iconic call for nationalism, republicanism, equal rights, liberty, and democracy. He suspended habeas corpus, and he averted British intervention. As the war progressed, he maneuvered to end slavery, issuing the Emancipation Proclamation of 1863. He was shot by John Wilkes Booth, an actor and Confederate sympathizer, on April 14, 1865, and died the following day. Abraham Lincoln is remembered as the United States' martyr hero. He is consistently ranked both by scholars and the public as one of the greatest U.S. presidents.

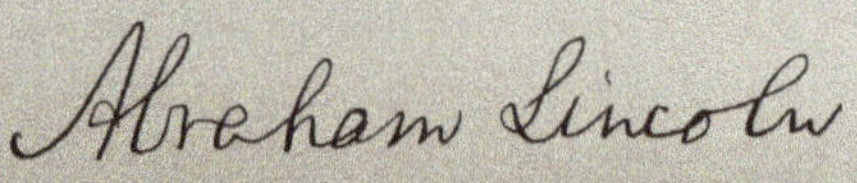

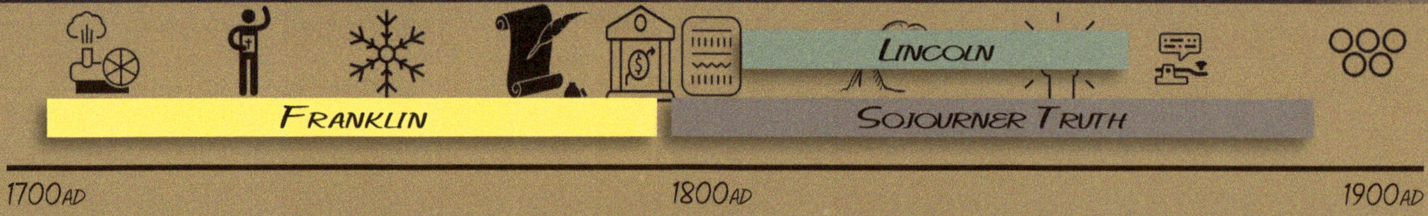